Burnt Balloons

Miss Riddle

Sometimes you just have to wade through the darkness.
You'll realize there's lights all around you.

Just because the lights have went out for now,
You're the magician who lights the flames.

Nothing external will do that for you.
Your outer life is the reflection of your inner life.

The darkness isn't something to be afraid of.
It's your own thoughts that are eating you,
not that the darkness consumed you.

All light is born out of darkness.
You have to get to his place to truly create for yourself.

I am my fathers daughter,
strong willed to the bone.
I am my fathers daughter,
nomad soul looking for my home.
I am my fathers daughter,
with a heart meant to roam.
I am my fathers daughter,
with a vast curiosity to the unknown.

Ambition eats apathy,
but depression will feast on
ambition like a demon in the night.

Whatever meaning you assign to life is the vibration and frequency that you will exist within.

I chose to transcend while you chose to descend.

Faltering fatalities were our biggest downfall;
for never speaking the truth.

We hid behind walls,
and all the armor and suits.

Happy is an emotion, content is a state.

You can not ever be consistently in one emotion,
you can achieve a constant state.

Perceptions control feelings.
Our perceptions are shaped by experiences.
Sometimes we have to learn to change what we
thought we knew to become the
phoenix that arises from the ashes.

I don't keep myself anywhere I can't provide value to.
I spent years learning who I am to know where I can fit.
It's not about what you can get from people;
it's about what you can give.

How do you tell where you should be placing your energy and time?
Take a look around you and see where there
is reciprocation with anything and everything in your life.
Reciprocation is how you're able to keep your
grass watered without it ever withering.

If you notice it's not mutual it is up to you to
Have some grace to delegate your path.

You know who your people are;
celebrate them.

I haven't wanted to turn the pages backwards in a really long time.

Regret and circling hatred prying towards me is shared by both parties
and there's nothing I can do.
But rebuild stone by stone, yet again.
You weren't supposed to ever be let in.

I knew from the start you had only a temporary mark,
but the taste of your lips like a fine aged wine;
full of melancholy and what would have never be called mine.

We're not much different you and I...
I wonder if either will learn to swallow pride.

I know you understood your part in the game,
was it worth not having your monsters slain?

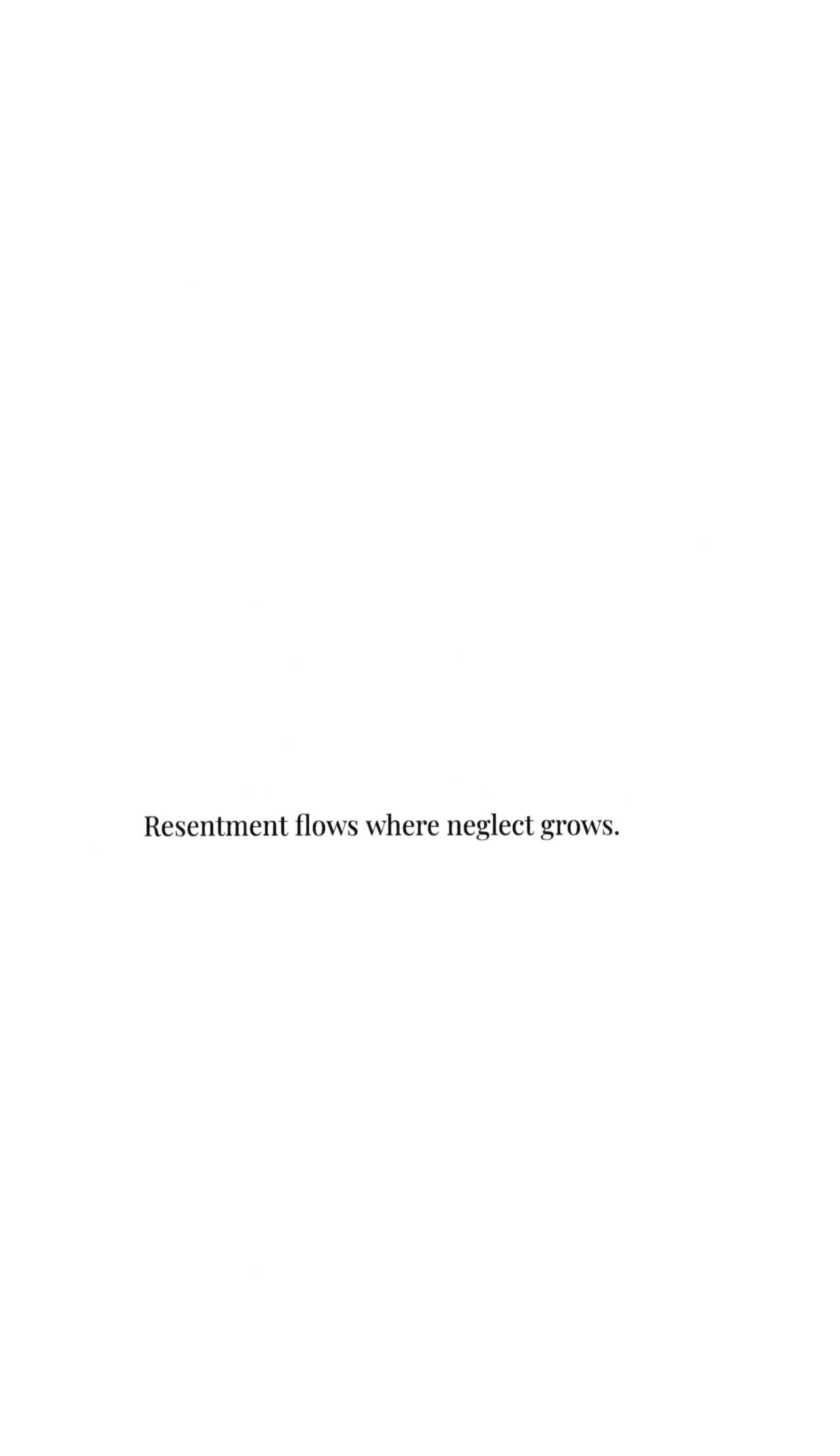

Resentment flows where neglect grows.

Being neglected in the ways I was while pouring
myself out to keep it together for you
created an unnecessary hole in my soul.

Was it really necessary to take out your gun and
unload the clip right into all
four chambers of this heart?

You want me to control what comes out of my mouth,
so you don't have to control your reactions...

Sweetheart,
I don't think you realize who I am.

You gaslit me into seeing your reality.

Tremendous work for a reality that's built on
anxiety and a desire to control everything.
This reality will break one day
no matter how well you build it up.

There are things I was supposed to teach you too.
You're not working on the right things inside.

It's only a matter of time.

When you heal they don't tell you that you're going to need to equip yourself for the fact that most people are not healed and how to deal with that.

We grasp onto nothing tightly,
afraid to see the truth.

Selfish greed, an incessant need;
would always make us lose.

Enough is enough.

It's time to change what you tolerate;
it obviously isn't working for you.

My biggest test I keep failing in life is learning
how to walk away with a heart full of love for someone else.

Willpower is just stubbornness dressed up.

You taught me that it's okay to be the
villain in someone else's story.

Just make sure you're never gonna want time with
me again if you do give me that title.

Villains wouldn't help you when you're drowning.

If you're gonna degrade my character
at least get the insults right.

Complaining without changing is just a pity party.

Just because nobody ever taught you about
personal responsibility, doesn't
mean that it doesn't exist.

We are the saviors we've been waiting for.

And there it was.

That moment we wait for when we know things have finally changed.

When that internal dialogue just isn't the same as before,
but it works immensely better for you.

Things may not appear to be different on the outside yet.

Baby steps are required for growth.

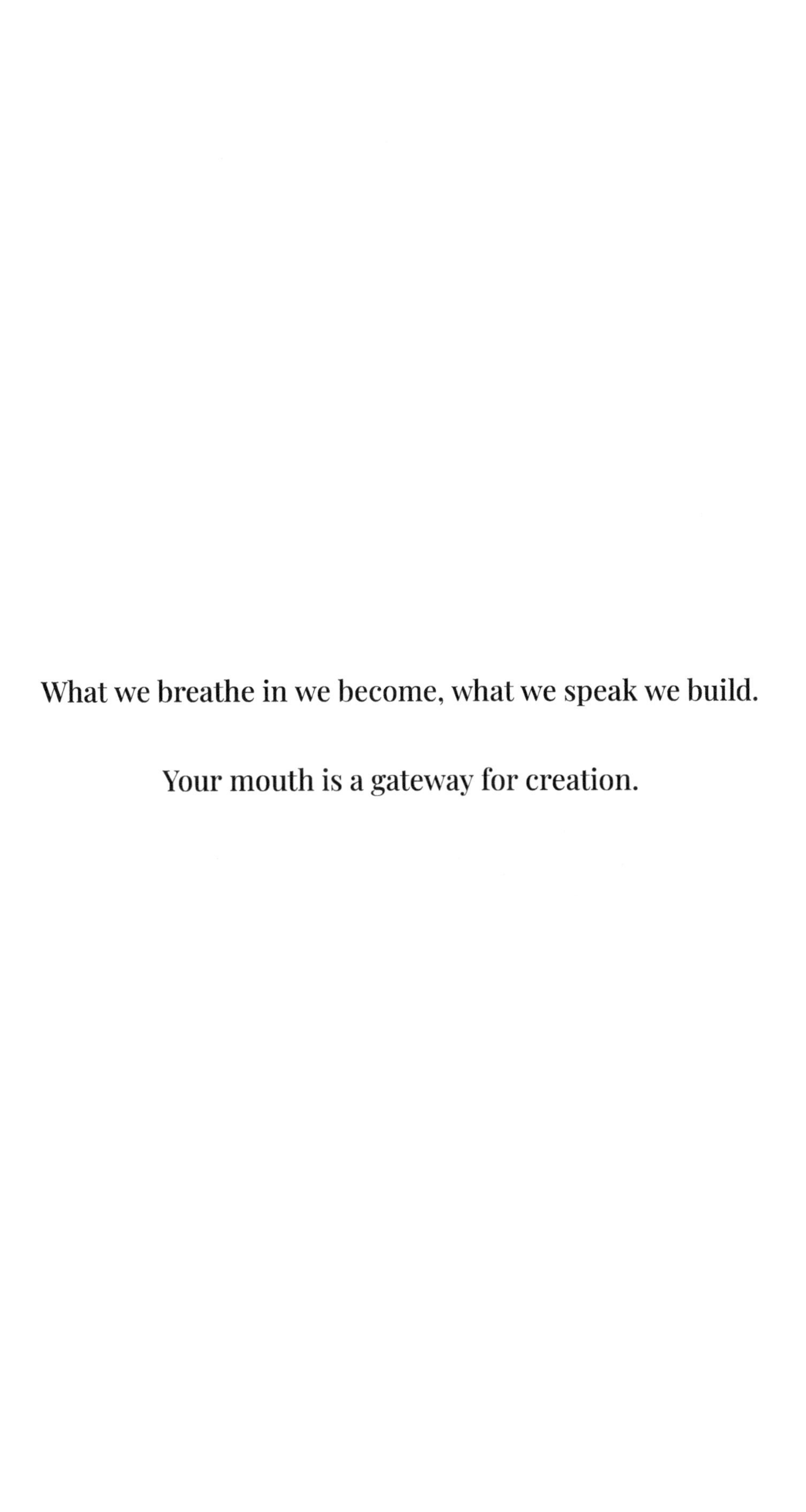

What we breathe in we become, what we speak we build.

Your mouth is a gateway for creation.

I want my existence to help people feel that they're not alone.

That no matter where they are in life or
what they're going through that you can look within,
make a choice and bring themselves to where they need to go.

It's never too late.

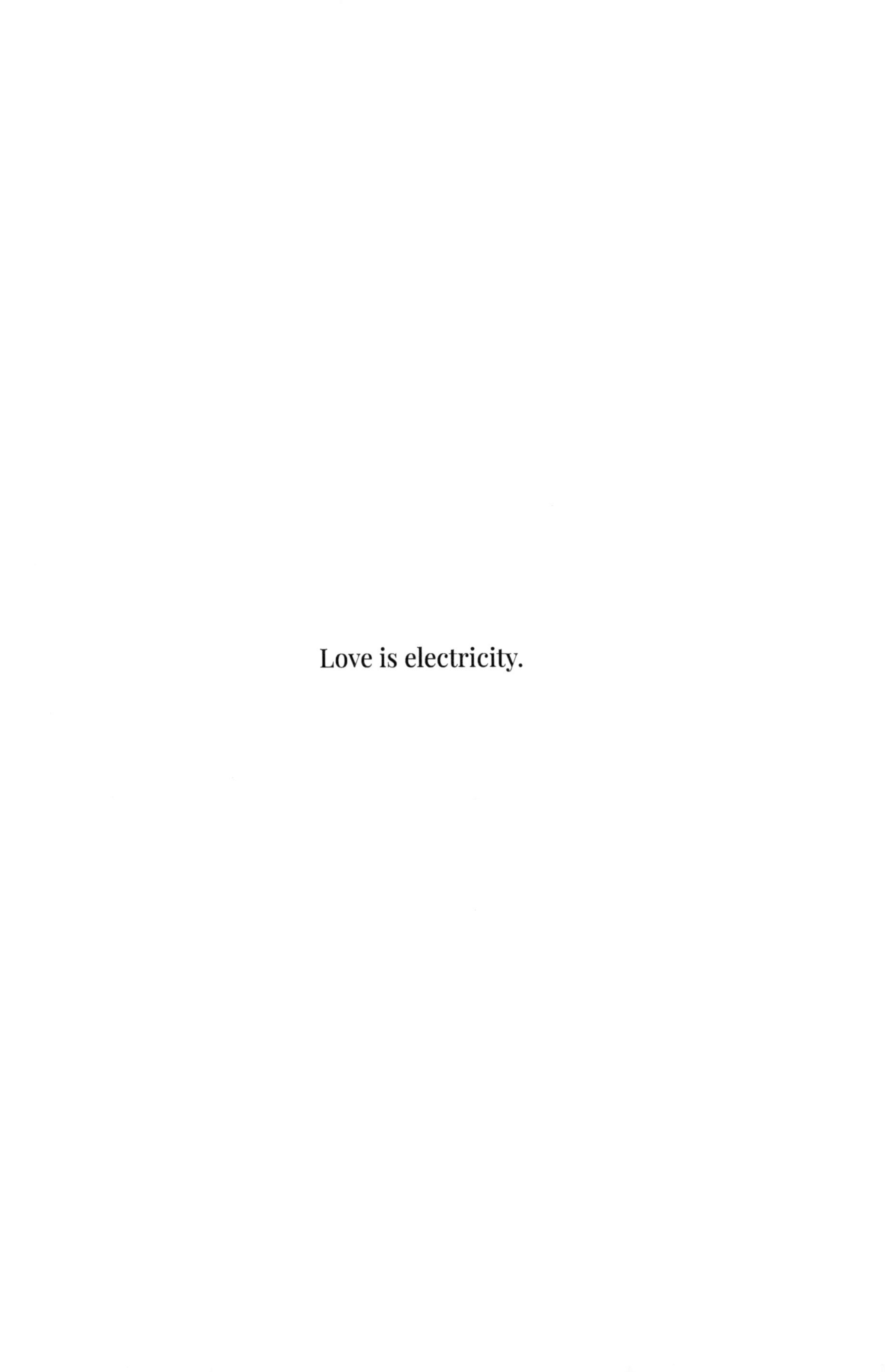

Love is electricity.

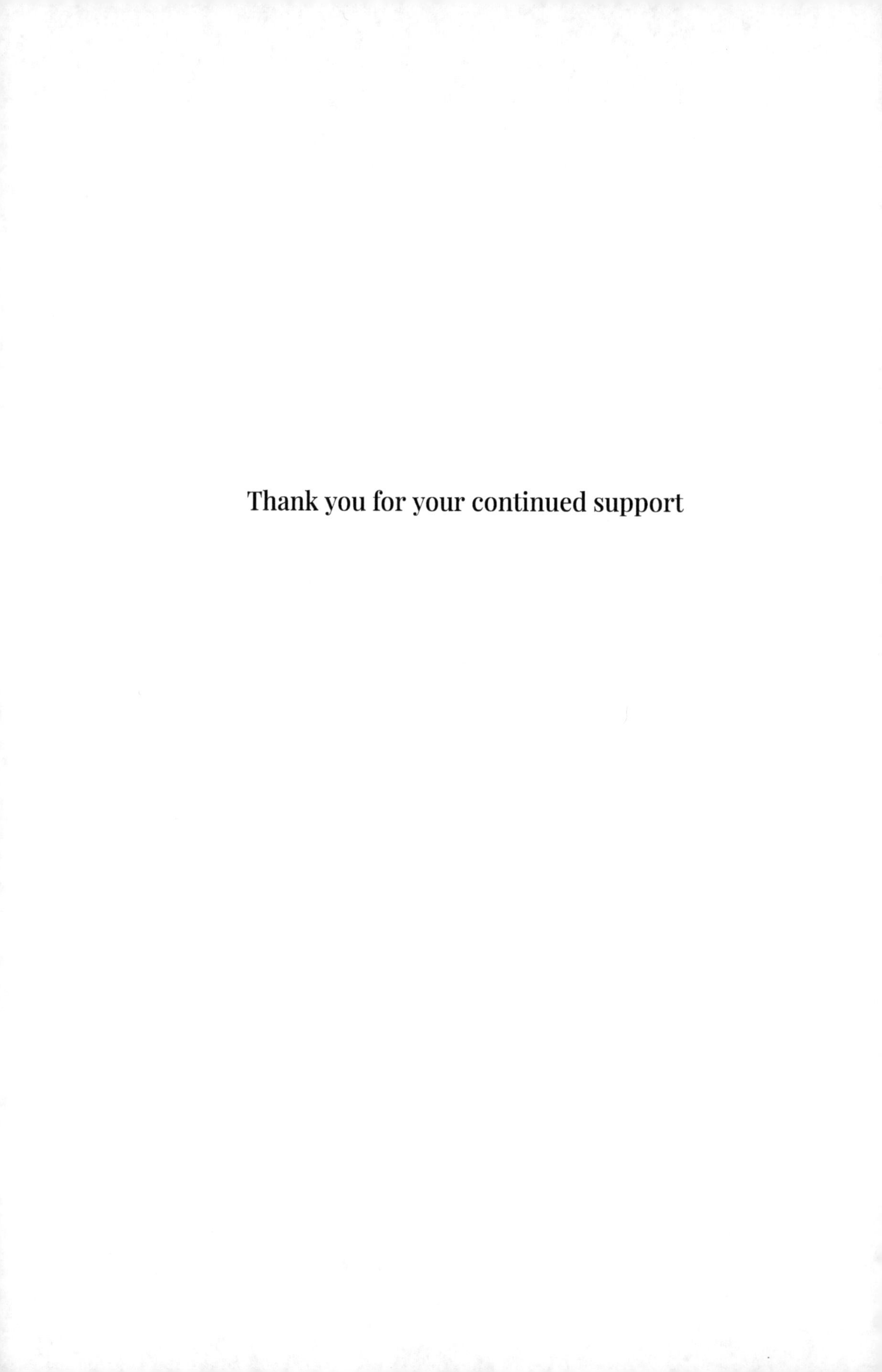
Thank you for your continued support

www.ingramcontent.com/pod-product-compliance
Lightning Source LLC
LaVergne TN
LVHW080629160826
845677LV00007B/1485

* 9 7 9 8 3 7 3 5 7 2 7 5 0 *